MEMORY

JOURNAL

Don't keep your memories locked away in your mind – share them through this journal and reflect on the things that have always stayed with you. Begin with some quick fire questions to kick-start your reflective thinking, then progress onto your family tree, early years and work life and more. When was the last time you thought about your childhood best friend? Think about the adventures that you used to get up to and reminisce about family holidays, family feuds and happy festive days all together. What do you remember about school? Did you behave? What was your first date like? Do you remember saying 'I love you' for the first time? Pour your heart and memories into this interactive journal and let your story live on for your loves ones to read.

MEMORY JOURNAL

Future PLC Quay House, The Ambury, Bath, BA1 1UA

Editorial
Editor **Rebecca Greig**
Art Editor **Katy Stokes**
Compiled by **Sarah Bankes & Briony Duguid**
Senior Art Editor **Andy Downes**
Head of Art & Design **Greg Whitaker**
Editorial Director **Jon White**

Cover images
Getty Images

Advertising
Media packs are available on request
Commercial Director **Clare Dove**

International
Head of Print Licensing **Rachel Shaw**
licensing@futurenet.com
www.futurecontenthub.com

Circulation
Head of Newstrade **Tim Mathers**

Production
Head of Production **Mark Constance**
Production Project Manager **Matthew Eglinton**
Advertising Production Manager **Joanne Crosby**
Digital Editions Controller **Jason Hudson**
Production Managers **Keely Miller, Nola Cokely, Vivienne Calvert, Fran Twentyman**

Printed in the UK

Distributed by Marketforce, 5 Churchill Place,
Canary Wharf, London, E14 5HU
www.marketforce.co.uk – For enquiries, please
email: mfcommunications@futurenet.com

Memory Journal Third Edition (LBZ5429)
© 2023 Future Publishing Limited

We are committed to only using magazine paper which is derived from responsibly managed, certified forestry and chlorine-free manufacture. The paper in this bookazine was sourced and produced from sustainable managed forests, conforming to strict environmental and socioeconomic standards.

All contents © 2023 Future Publishing Limited or published under licence. All rights reserved. No part of this magazine may be used, stored, transmitted or reproduced in any way without the prior written permission of the publisher. Future Publishing Limited (company number 2008885) is registered in England and Wales. Registered office: Quay House, The Ambury, Bath BA1 1UA. All information contained in this publication is for information only and is, as far as we are aware, correct at the time of going to press. Future cannot accept any responsibility for errors or inaccuracies in such information. You are advised to contact manufacturers and retailers directly with regard to the price of products/services referred to in this publication. Apps and websites mentioned in this publication are not under our control. We are not responsible for their contents or any other changes or updates to them. This magazine is fully independent and not affiliated in any way with the companies mentioned herein.

Future plc is a public company quoted on the London Stock Exchange (symbol: FUTR)
www.futureplc.com

Chief executive **Jon Steinberg**
Non-executive chairman **Richard Huntingford**
Chief financial officer **Penny Ladkin-Brand**

Tel +44 (0)1225 442 244

WHAT IS

MEMORY?

OUR MEMORIES ARE A RECORD OF OUR LIVES AND EVERYTHING WE HAVE LEARNED FROM IT

LET'S THINK ABOUT MEMORY

EVERY MOMENT BECOMES A MEMORY INSTANTLY,
BUT WHAT EXACTLY GIVES SOME OF THEM VALUE?

FUTURE

Our brains are not computers. While we store massive amounts of data within them, they're not infallible when it comes to remembering everything we learn and experience. There are very few of us who accurately remember every single thing that has happened to us.

✶ TYPES OF MEMORY ✶

When we talk about 'memory' it's important to note that we're not talking about one massive operation. There are so many types of memory, and these can be broken down further into other sub-categories — this is totally ignoring the molecular stuff that's going on in our brains as we form them!

You may have heard of short-term memories. This is essentially your working memory, with a recall period of just a few seconds to a minute without rehearsal. These are temporary memories that help us with decision-making and general behaviour. Something like telephone number recall is a good example of short-term memory. Our short-term or working memory has limited capacity, but we can use techniques to help us remember more. For example, we can break up numbers into smaller chunks such as area codes to make them easier to recall.

Long-term memory is the stage of memory where information is held for a longer period of time. It is here that we store large quantities of data from throughout our lives. We can use the telephone example above to prove this. We often remember telephone numbers from our past as we have logged them in our long-term memory with constant repetition.

We can use the term declarative (or explicit) memory to classify the memories that are consciously stored and ready for recollection. This grouping can be split further into semantic and episodic memory sub-divisions. Semantic memory is our

THE DRY STUFF

In short, memory is the acquisition, storage, retention and retrieval of information in our brains. We often talk about memory as being very personal and related to our experiences and life stories. However, memory is not just our recollection of the past. It is also the process our brains use to learn. For example, when we learn a new language we use memory. Our brains encode, store and retrieve this information in many ways.

factual knowledge i.e. things you've remembered for a test. Episodic memories are our memories of specific times, like what happened last time you saw someone. We also have episodic memories, which are specific just to us throughout our lives.

Procedural (or implicit) memory has everything to do with our motor skills, how we learn to use our bodies or other objects and instruments. Interestingly enough, the more we access these procedural memories, the faster you can perform the task — practice makes perfect! New memories aren't being formed when these are being accessed — you're just strengthening the existing ones.

✳ RECALL vs RECOGNITION ✳

There are a number of ways in which our brains retrieve information from memory. Recall, recognition and re-learning are three such ways. Recall reproduces the information and can be done in a 'free' fashion. You may be asked to remember as much information as you can in no particular order. Recognition is the retrieval method that requires you to find the 'right' answer in a sea of alternatives — like a multiple choice quiz. Re-learning is exactly what it sounds like — learning information again.

Now memory is not just the type that scientists and psychologists use to classify brain waves. It is a key part of what makes us who we are. In terms of looking after ourselves, we must also look after our memory. It is hard to overstate the importance of sleep to help us store, consolidate and recall memories. Apart from making it harder for us to focus (and harder to learn), chronic sleep deprivation can also lead to false memories.

✳ WHY WE FORGET ✳

In TV and films, memory loss is often triggered and reversed by a blow to the head. In real life, it is much less dramatic. Memories simply get weaker over time. This can be caused by something as common as absent mindedness, which is when a memory fades due to lack of attention.

"MEMORY IS THE TREASURY AND
GUARDIAN OF ALL THINGS"
- CICERO

In the last 20 years a new kind of memory loss has cropped up called digital amnesia. Many adults cannot remember their current phone numbers, or those of their family or friends but have no problem recalling their childhood home number! Many academics believe this has come from a reliance on technology. We simply don't have to remember numbers when it's all too easy to look them up! In a way, we're outsourcing many of our memories to technology and using it as an extension of our brains.

There are a whole raft of memory problems that can be diagnosed by medical professionals and it's very common that memory loss increases as we age.

Interestingly, if an event or experience is highly emotionally charged we're unlikely to forget it. This is called the memory enhancement effect.

Learning under stress decreases memory recall. Studies have shown that stress often distracts people during a memory encoding process. Whereas with assisted learning — chewing gum, drinking coffee, wearing perfume while studying while you learn — you can trick your brain into remembering with these associations.

✴ KEEPING YOUR MEMORY ✴ STRONG AND HEALTHY

The perfect mix for keeping your memory skills sharp is a good diet, healthy sleep habits, low stress and memory exercises! Brain teasers, puzzles and memory training games are perfect ways to keep your memory in shape.

LET ME

TELL YOU A STORY

SHARING MEMORIES CAN HELP
REINFORCE BONDS

Whether we realise it or not, we're strengthening bonds with others every time we reminisce, share memories or engage in collaborative storytelling. When we share sad memories, we can be looking for sympathy or to cast ourselves in a sympathetic light. When we share memories and stories of our achievements we may want to spread our joy or to show how capable we are.

Sharing memories can help our own memory as we age. Experiments undertaken with long-term couples sharing memories showed that those who remembered with their parters found it much easier to recall the whole story, whereas those reminiscing alone struggled.

✶ GROUP IDENTITY ✶

Shared memories form group identities, from reinforcing family bonds to agreeing how history is to be remembered. Researchers often refer to this kind of group memory as being created by remembering teams. Everyone contributes and this actually creates more memories. However, this can break down when there are family disagreements or marital breakups. Established memories can then be torn apart and reinterpreted to highlight 'wrongs' whether these are real or imagined.

Group identities are often wider than those of just families. Folklore of specific areas or natural features are frequent around the world. This sort of group

SOCIAL CONTAGION

The phrase "social contagion" is used to describe how we can wrongly add information that has been provided to us by other people into our own memories. We often feel that our memories should line up with those of family, friends and colleagues. Occasionally, we fully believe other people's recollections of the past to the disbenefit of our own memories.

memory, such as stories of fairies attached to springs, is a kind of folk memory. This is a term to describe folklore about past events that are passed from generation to generation. Folklore varies from fairytales as they are presented as fact.

To widen the 'group memory' idea even further, we can talk about national (or even international) memory. We take part in collective memory when we mark

FOLKLORE AND FACTS

There are many myths that have been passed on from generation to generation via oral storytelling. There is often a fascinating crossover with science in many folkloric myths. The native people of Australia retell stories of the bunyip, a large creature that lurks in water (a kind of evil spirit). While descriptions of bunyips vary in stories they have been associated by modern scientists with gigantic extinct marsupials that have been discovered in ancient waterways.

two minutes of silence for Remembrance day or other significant anniversaries. Collective memories are important in understanding how 'we' as a group, nation or species view ourselves and our past. While showing respect for those we have lost at war, we show as a people that we are united in our belief that this was a tragic event and should never happen again.

✱ PERSONAL IDENTITY ✱

Sharing memories are not just designed to bond us to those around us. We also use storytelling to strengthen how we view ourselves as we work on how we present ourselves to others. We use memories as a way of documenting ourselves to our loved ones and the ones we come into contact with. We present our ideal self to them. Think back to memories of people you know. Is the picture you have of them formed by your own first person interactions with them, or is it part of a tapestry of what you've experienced and what you have been told?

> "EVERY HAPPY MEMORY CREATED FOR A CHILD
> IS ANOTHER TREASURE OF A LIFETIME"
> - DONNA MARIE

✴ TEACHING SKILLS ✴
TO GENERATIONS TO COME

Humans use memories to teach our children how to remember. When parents and carers talk to babies they work on the who/how/why/what of events, developing memory and encouraging children to tell stories. Parents can guide this kind of retelling, not inform little ones of what happened, which allows children to contribute. Reminiscing with children can help to navigate difficult memories and the emotions that accompany them. Families sharing openly and emotionally can often see older children with higher levels of self-esteem and a more positive attitude towards adversity.

✴ GETTING IT WRONG? ✴

We all get memories wrong. Details can be muddled and arguments can develop over who got it right. While contradictions can shut down conversations, we should take the opportunity to learn instead that everyone has their own perspective. Accuracy is not the goal of memory and sharing memories. We may not like it if someone retells a cherished memory differently, as our memories make us who we are. If something is fundamentally different in a story are we still the same person formed by those memories?

TIME FOR REFLECTION

IT'S IMPORTANT TO TAKE TIME TO REFLECT ON OUR MEMORIES AND THE EFFECT OF EACH MOMENT

We can push this review into the sphere of reflection by using conscious effort in thinking. Make sure you use your self-awareness, your experiences and your unique view. This kind of growth mindset helps with overall self-improvement. Work on learning from your experiences and you will begin to understand how you think and why you take the actions you do. Try to view reflection as empowering. You are in control of your decisions and life is not a cycle. With mindful self-reflection you can break any patterns of unhelpful behaviour.

REFLECTIVE PERSONALITIES MAY FIND THIS EASY

There are many people out there that can (and do) work on a thought for days and days, dissecting it and (sometimes) overthinking it. You may be an overly reflective person if you struggle to make decisions because you enjoy the work of thinking.

✴ LEARNING HOW ✴

Remember, you are not alone. You can reflect with others whether by writing or speaking. Many social psychologists suggest that learning occurs most effectively when thoughts are pulled out of our brain and put into language, so talk it out.

Take time to journal about every day activities and events, and reflect on what you have learned from them. What could you do differently if the same thing happens again? Remember to give yourself credit when you highlight something you believe you have done well! Work on explaining situations and actions fully. Be honest with yourself. Reflect on the past but also focus on how you can work on how this affects the future.

There are a few different ways to structure your self-reflection. Two major models of reflection are that of Kolb and Schön. Kolb's learning cycle focuses on relating your experience, objectively observing and reflecting, and then working on developing new ideas with an aim to test new ideas in practice. Schön focuses on two types of reflection: one during and one after an experience. In action we focus on the experience (thinking on our feet, thinking what comes next, acting immediately). In post-event reflection we think about what has happened and analyse what we would do differently.

When mindfully self-reflecting, focus on the three Ws to help focus your journalling; *What happened? What was important about the event? What have I learned?*

✳ WHY IS THIS IMPORTANT? ✳

While self-reflection helps us to avoid the pitfalls we have fallen prey to in the past, it also has a number of additional benefits. This kind of work builds self-awareness, creative thinking skills, and helps boost engagement with you work, school and life. We use self-reflection as a form of personal appraisal — much like a development review at work. We can use a self-reflection process to remind us to focus on the important stuff and seek out what really matters in our lives.

✳ WHY DO WE NOT DO IT? ✳

While reflecting you may find yourself asking why you haven't done this before. There are numerous reasons we avoid this kind of self-analysis. Many people don't reflect as they find the process difficult. Reflecting on times when you haven't been successful in an endeavour is an anathema to some. Many people just don't like the process, or haven't found the right process! Try a few different ways to self-reflect: talk, write or structure your process to suit you uniquely. Other people don't like having to face results that may not be glowing, but remember, this is how we ensure that we succeed in the future. Result-driven people can feel that reflection is a waste of time. They feel that they should be doing something and not working on the theory or looking back!

THE FIVE Rs OF REFLECTION

The five elements of this framework for deep reflection are Reporting, Responding, Reasoning, Relating and Reconstructing. Reporting is just that — dispassionate facts. Responding focuses on the emotional intelligence we bring to an experience and relating allows us to draw on our knowledge. Reasoning is the explanation, and reconstructing focuses us on the future. We're making complete sense of what we have learned through experience.

"

GOD GAVE US MEMORY SO THAT WE MIGHT HAVE ROSES IN DECEMBER

— J.M. BARRIE

RECORD YOUR MEMORIES

DON'T KEEP YOUR MEMORIES LOCKED AWAY IN
YOUR MIND – WRITE THEM DOWN AND SHARE THEM

QUICK

QUESTIONS

KEEP YOUR MEMORIES ALIVE BY
WRITING IT ALL DOWN — FOR
YOU AND FUTURE GENERATIONS

✷ ABOUT ME ✷

FIRST NAME

LAST NAME AND MAIDEN NAME

DATE OF BIRTH

BIRTH PLACE

HEIGHT

EYE COLOUR

HAIR COLOUR

MOST DISTINGUISHING FEATURE

OCCUPATION

ATTACH A BABY
PHOTO HERE

"MEMORY IS THE TREASURY
AND GUARDIAN OF
ALL THINGS
- CICERO

✴ FIRST ✴ EXPERIENCES

 WHAT WAS YOUR FIRST WORD?

 WHAT WAS THE FIRST MOVIE YOU WATCHED?

 WHAT WAS THE FIRST ALBUM YOU BOUGHT?

 HOW OLD WERE YOU WHEN YOU HAD YOUR FIRST KISS?

 WHO WAS THE FIRST PERSON YOU TOOK FOR DINNER?

 WHAT WAS THE FIRST BAR YOU LEGALLY WENT TO?

 AT WHAT AGE DID YOU FIRST TRY ALCOHOL?

 WHERE DID YOU GO ON YOUR FIRST FIRST DATE?

"ONE PERSON'S GREATEST REGRET IS ANOTHER PERSON'S GREATEST MEMORY"

— ANGELA LAM TURPIN

✦ FIRST ✦
EXPERIENCES

 WHERE DID YOU GO ON YOUR FIRST AIRPLANE FLIGHT?

 WHERE WAS THE FIRST COUNTRY YOU VISITED?

 WHAT WAS THE FIRST CONCERT YOU WENT TO?

 HOW OLD WERE YOU WHEN YOU FIRST FELL IN LOVE?

 WHO WAS YOUR FIRST CRUSH?

 WHAT WAS YOUR FIRST PET? DID IT HAVE A NAME?

 WHAT WAS YOUR FIRST CAR?

 WHAT WAS YOUR FIRST JOB?

CHANGE THE FONT

Most things we look to remember are written in the same few fonts. If you have access to the raw information, try to change it to a more 'difficult' to read font. This engages deeper processing strategies. You're working on understanding the words, not just skimming!

✶ QUICK ✶
QUESTIONS

 WHAT WAS YOUR FAVOURITE CHOCOLATE AS A CHILD?

 WHAT WAS YOUR FAVOURITE TOY AS A CHILD?

 WHAT WAS YOUR CHILDHOOD BEST FRIEND'S NAME?

 HOW MANY SIBLINGS DO YOU HAVE?

 HOW MANY PEOPLE ARE IN YOUR IMMEDIATE FAMILY?

 HOW DID YOU GET TO SCHOOL?

 WHAT IS YOUR FAVOURITE COLOUR?

 AS A CHILD, WHAT DID YOUR PARENTS DO FOR WORK?

WOLFGANG AMADEUS MOZART SAVES RARE PIECE

At the age of 14 Mozart heard a piece of music once and was able to transcribe it from his memory. The piece, Miserere mei, was composed by Gregorio Allegri could only be performed in the Sistine Chapel in the Vatican City until Mozart wrote it down!

✶ QUICK QUESTIONS ✶

 WHAT WAS YOUR FAVOURITE SONG AS A CHILD?

 WHAT'S YOUR LUCKY NUMBER?

 WHO HAS ALWAYS MADE YOU LAUGH?

 WHAT IS THE FARTHEST YOU HAVE EVER TRAVELLED?

 HOW LONG WAS YOUR LONGEST CAR JOURNEY?

 HAVE YOU EVER BROKEN ANY BONES?

 WHAT WERE YOUR FAVOURITE CHILDHOOD SHOWS?

 DO YOU HAVE A FAVOURITE INSPIRATIONAL QUOTE?

"I HAVE A POOR MEMORY FOR NAMES; BUT I SELDOM REMEMBER A FACE"
– W.C. FIELDS

✦ QUICK ✦ QUESTIONS

 HOW LONG WAS YOUR LONGEST TRAIN JOURNEY?

 WHAT COMPETITIONS HAVE YOU WON?

 WHAT DID YOU TREASURE MOST AS A CHILD?

 WHAT MAGAZINE OR COMIC DID YOU READ AS A CHILD?

 WHAT WAS YOUR FAVOURITE FILM AS A CHILD?

 WHAT WAS YOUR FAVOURITE SPORT AS A CHILD?

 WHAT WAS YOUR FAVOURITE PLACE AS A CHILD?

 NAME YOUR FAVOURITE ADULT AS A CHILD.

"A GOOD LIFE IS A COLLECTION OF HAPPY MEMORIES"
- DENIS WAITLEY

✦ QUICK QUESTIONS ✦

 WHO WERE YOU AFRAID OF AS A CHILD?

 WHAT WERE YOU GOOD AT AS A CHILD?

 WHAT WAS YOUR FAVOURITE PLAYGROUND GAME?

 WHAT DID YOU WANT TO BE WHEN YOU GREW UP?

 WERE YOU NAMED AFTER ANYONE?

 DID YOU TAKE AFTER ANYONE?

 WHAT DIDN'T YOU LIKE ABOUT YOURSELF AS A CHILD?

 WHAT DID YOU LIKE ABOUT YOURSELF?

TAKE A MENTAL PICTURE

Have you ever left your keys somewhere and then forgotten where you put them? Try making mental notes when you do things. So next time you leave drop your keys, make a point of saying to yourself, they're next to the fruit bowl. Oddly enough, this will help you remember.

✦ QUICK ✦
QUESTIONS

 WRITE DOWN THE FIVE MOST MEMORABLE PLACES YOU HAVE VISITED.

1 ||
2 ||
3 ||
4 ||
5 ||

WRITE DOWN FIVE OF YOUR FAVOURITE FOODS AS A CHILD.

1 ||
2 ||
3 ||
4 ||
5 ||

NISCHAL NARAYANAM, SUPER REMEMBER-ER!

Nischal, from India, claimed his first world record in remembering at the age of ten! He remembered 225 objects and recalled them in around 12 minutes. He followed this at age 12 by memorising 132 digits in a minute!

✦ QUICK QUESTIONS ✦

 WRITE DOWN FIVE HOBBIES YOU HAVE TAKEN UP THROUGHOUT YOUR LIFE.

1.
2.
3.
4.
5.

 WRITE DOWN FIVE OF YOUR FAVOURITE BANDS OR ARTISTS FROM THROUGHOUT YOUR LIFE.

1.
2.
3.
4.
5.

"COLLECT MOMENTS, NOT THINGS."
- PAOLO COELHOS

QUICK QUESTIONS

WRITE DOWN FIVE OF THE BEST OR MOST MEMORABLE PRESENTS YOU HAVE RECEIVED.

1.
2.
3.
4.
5.

WRITE DOWN FIVE OF YOUR FAVOURITE BOOKS.

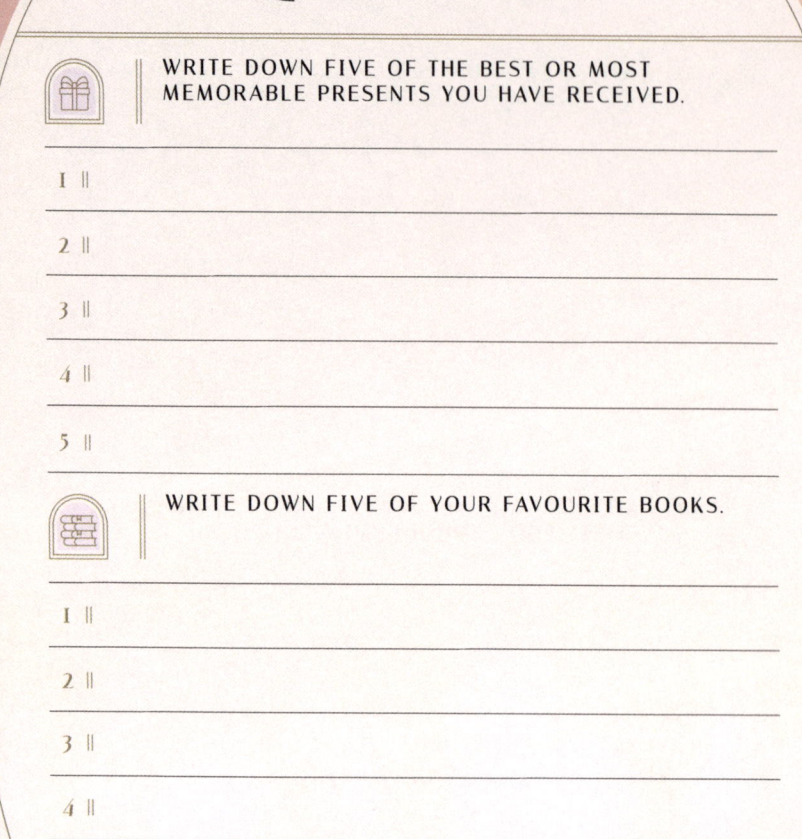

1.
2.
3.
4.
5.

"A GOOD MEMORY IS ONE TRAINED TO FORGET THE TRIVIAL"
– CLIFTON FADIMAN

QUICK QUESTIONS

WRITE DOWN FIVE OF YOUR FAVOURITE SONGS OF ALL TIME.

1.
2.
3.
4.
5.

WRITE DOWN THE TOP FIVE DAYS OF YOUR LIFE.

1.
2.
3.
4.
5.

WHAT IS MEMORY?

We have three functions of memory; acquisition (how we imprint on our brain), consolidation (transferring information from short-term to long-term memory), and recall (retrieving the information for future use).

LET'S TRIGGER

YOUR MEMORIES

ASSOCIATION IS A POWERFUL MEMORY AID, AS WELL AS AN EFFECTIVE LEARNING TOOL

WHAT MEMORIES DO YOU ASSOCIATE WITH SPRING?

_____
_____
_____
_____
_____
_____
_____

WHAT MEMORIES DO YOU ASSOCIATE WITH SUMMER?

_____
_____
_____
_____
_____
_____
_____
_____

WHAT MEMORIES DO YOU ASSOCIATE WITH WINTER?

_____
_____
_____
_____
_____
_____
_____

WHAT MEMORIES DO YOU ASSOCIATE WITH AUTUMN?

_____
_____
_____
_____
_____
_____
_____

> **MEMORIES OF OUR LIVES, OF OUR WORKS AND OUR DEEDS WILL CONTINUE IN OTHERS**
>
> – ROSA PARKS

WHEN YOU SMELL PINE NEEDLES WHAT MEMORIES COME TO MIND?

WHEN YOU SMELL SUN CREAM WHAT MEMORIES COME TO MIND?

_____

_____

_____

_____

_____

_____

WHEN YOU SMELL CUT GRASS WHAT MEMORIES COME TO MIND?

_____

_____

_____

_____

_____

_____

> **TROUBLE REMEMBERING?**
>
> If you find things slipping your mind, try a quick mindfulness exercise. Take a few minutes to pay full attention to what it is that you're doing. Whether this is reading, eating or relaxing. Pay full attention to the moment.

WHEN YOU SMELL CINNAMON WHAT MEMORIES COME TO MIND?

_____
_____
_____
_____
_____
_____

WHEN YOU SMELL STALE BEER WHAT MEMORIES COME TO MIND?

_____
_____
_____
_____
_____
_____

WHEN YOU SMELL PETROL WHAT MEMORIES COME TO MIND?

"

NO MEMORY IS EVER ALONE,

IT'S AT THE END OF A TRAIL OF MEMORIES,

A DOZEN TRAILS THAT EACH HAVE THEIR OWN ASSOCIATIONS

— LOUIS L'AMOUR

WHEN YOU SMELL PENCIL ERASERS WHAT MEMORIES COME TO MIND?

_____
_____
_____
_____
_____
_____
_____

WHEN YOU SMELL BLEACH WHAT MEMORIES COME TO MIND?

_____
_____
_____
_____
_____
_____
_____

WHEN YOU SMELL ORANGE PEEL WHAT MEMORIES COME TO MIND?

_____

_____

_____

_____

_____

_____

_____

WHEN YOU SMELL COFFEE WHAT MEMORIES COME TO MIND?

_____

_____

_____

_____

_____

_____

_____

WHICH SENSE?

Has a scent ever transported you back in time? Odor-evoked autobiographical memory is very common! Smells and memories are filed closely in the brain: smells go to the olfactory bulb and memories are held in the hippocampus.

WHEN YOU SMELL BURNT TOAST WHAT MEMORIES COME TO MIND?

WHEN YOU GO ON A PLANE, WHAT MEMORIES COME TO MIND?

WALK AROUND YOUR HOUSE UNTIL YOU SPOT AN OBJECT THAT TRIGGERS MEMORIES FOR YOU.

The phone that rang to tell you about someone's death, the quilt that used to belong to your grandmother, the dress from the office Christmas party. Pick the one object that really hits a nerve. Write about the memories and emotions the object triggers.

GET MOVING!

Exercise goes a long way to improving our memory as oxygen levels and blood flow to our brain is increased. While exercising your muscles you're also growing blood vessels in your brain (which, in a way is like a big muscle!)

47 / *LET'S TRIGGER YOUR MEMORIES*

WHEN YOU GO SWIMMING, WHAT MEMORIES COME TO MIND?

_____
_____
_____
_____
_____
_____
_____

WHEN YOU GO TO THE BEACH, WHAT MEMORIES COME TO MIND?

_____
_____
_____
_____
_____
_____
_____
_____

"

LET YOUR MEMORY BE YOUR TRAVEL BAG

— ALEKSANDR SOLZHENITSYN

WHEN YOU WEAR FORMAL ATTIRE WHAT MEMORIES COME TO MIND?

WHEN YOU WEAR JEANS, WHAT MEMORIES COME TO MIND?

_____
_____
_____
_____
_____
_____
_____

> **THAT'S A LOT OF DATA!**
>
> According to Paul Reber, a psychology professor at Northwestern University, our brains have the capacity to store around 2.5 petabytes of data. That's three million hours of TV, which would take 300 years to play!

WHEN YOU GO ON A TRAIN, WHAT MEMORIES COME TO MIND?

_____
_____
_____
_____
_____
_____
_____
_____
_____

WHEN YOU GO TO CHURCH, WHAT MEMORIES COME TO MIND?

_____
_____
_____
_____
_____
_____

WHEN YOU GO TO A CEMETERY, WHAT MEMORIES COME TO MIND?

_____
_____
_____
_____
_____
_____

REMOVE THE DISTRACTIONS

If you're asked to remember certain details about something you've just watched, close your eyes! Research has shown that by removing visual distractions you can be much more accurate in your recall.

WHEN YOU GO TO A PLAY PARK, WHAT MEMORIES COME TO MIND?

"

ANYTHING THAT TRIGGERS

GOOD

MEMORIES CAN'T BE ALL

BAD

— ADAM WEST

WHEN YOU GO TO THE THEATRE, WHAT MEMORIES COME TO MIND?

_____

_____

_____

_____

_____

> **HOW WE LEARN AND MEMORISE**
>
> Visual learning is real. A large percentage of people are visual learners; visual aids assist them in retaining and understanding information. This is backed up in the fact that we retain around one-fifth of what we hear!

WHEN YOU GO ICE SKATING, WHAT MEMORIES COME TO MIND?

_____

_____

_____

_____

_____

_____

_____

_____

WHEN YOU VISIT YOUR HOME TOWN, WHAT MEMORIES COME TO MIND?

_____
_____
_____
_____
_____
_____
_____

WHEN YOU DRIVE ON THE MOTORWAY, WHAT MEMORIES COME TO MIND?

_____
_____
_____
_____
_____
_____
_____

> **SLEEP!**
> Experts recommend between seven and nine hours sleep for adults to assist good memory. Any more or less can affect the effectiveness of your memory consolidation. Many sleep disorders also have associated memory problems, like insomnia and narcolepsy.

WHEN YOU TASTE CHOCOLATE, WHAT MEMORIES COME TO MIND?

FAMILY TREE

KEEPING A RECORD OF YOUR FAMILY HISTORY CAN GIVE YOU A STRONGER SENSE OF SELF

✳ MY PARENTS ✳

PARENT A
- NAME
- DATE OF BIRTH
- BIRTH PLACE
- EYE COLOUR
- HAIR COLOUR

PARENT B
- NAME
- DATE OF BIRTH
- BIRTH PLACE
- EYE COLOUR
- HAIR COLOUR

STEP PARENT A
- NAME
- DATE OF BIRTH
- BIRTH PLACE
- EYE COLOUR
- HAIR COLOUR

STEP PARENT B
- NAME
- DATE OF BIRTH
- BIRTH PLACE
- EYE COLOUR
- HAIR COLOUR

✶ MY SIBLINGS ✶

SIBLING A

NAME

DATE OF BIRTH

BIRTH PLACE

EYE COLOUR

HAIR COLOUR

SIBLING B

NAME

DATE OF BIRTH

BIRTH PLACE

EYE COLOUR

HAIR COLOUR

SIBLING C

NAME

DATE OF BIRTH

BIRTH PLACE

EYE COLOUR

HAIR COLOUR

SIBLING D

NAME

DATE OF BIRTH

BIRTH PLACE

EYE COLOUR

HAIR COLOUR

✶ MY GRANDPARENTS ✶

GRANDPARENT A

NAME

DATE OF BIRTH

BIRTH PLACE

EYE COLOUR

HAIR COLOUR

GRANDPARENT A

NAME

DATE OF BIRTH

BIRTH PLACE

EYE COLOUR

HAIR COLOUR

GRANDPARENT B

NAME

DATE OF BIRTH

BIRTH PLACE

EYE COLOUR

HAIR COLOUR

GRANDPARENT B

NAME

DATE OF BIRTH

BIRTH PLACE

EYE COLOUR

HAIR COLOUR

✶ MY CHILDREN ✶

CHILD A

NAME

DATE OF BIRTH

BIRTH PLACE

EYE COLOUR

HAIR COLOUR

CHILD B

NAME

DATE OF BIRTH

BIRTH PLACE

EYE COLOUR

HAIR COLOUR

CHILD C

NAME

DATE OF BIRTH

BIRTH PLACE

EYE COLOUR

HAIR COLOUR

CHILD D

NAME

DATE OF BIRTH

BIRTH PLACE

EYE COLOUR

HAIR COLOUR

OTHER IMPORTANT FAMILY MEMBERS

FAMILY MEMBER A

NAME

DATE OF BIRTH

BIRTH PLACE

EYE COLOUR

HAIR COLOUR

FAMILY MEMBER B

NAME

DATE OF BIRTH

BIRTH PLACE

EYE COLOUR

HAIR COLOUR

FAMILY MEMBER C

NAME

DATE OF BIRTH

BIRTH PLACE

EYE COLOUR

HAIR COLOUR

FAMILY MEMBER D

NAME

DATE OF BIRTH

BIRTH PLACE

EYE COLOUR

HAIR COLOUR

- GREAT GRANDPARENT A
- GREAT GRANDPARENT B
  - GRANDPARENT A
- GREAT GRANDPARENT A
- GREAT GRANDPARENT B
  - GRANDPARENT B
- GREAT GRANDPARENT A
- GREAT GRANDPARENT B
  - GRANDPARENT A
- GREAT GRANDPARENT A
- GREAT GRANDPARENT B
  - GRANDPARENT B

OUR FAMILY TREE

- PARENT A
- PARENT B

- SIBLING
- SIBLING
- ME
- SIBLING
- SIBLING

WRITE ABOUT THE EARLIEST FAMILY
HOLIDAY THAT YOU CAN REMEMBER.

THE THING MY GRANPARENTS USED TO TELL ME MOST OFTEN WAS...

THE FONDEST MEMORY OF MY GRANDPARENTS IS...

WHERE WAS I GOING?

Psychologists led by Gabriel Radvansky at the University of Notre Dame found that doorways are often to blame when we forget what we were doing! Moving through a doorway assists our brains in 'filing episodic memories'.

67 / *FAMILY TREE*

THE MOST IMPORTANT LESSON THAT MY PARENT TAUGHT ME WAS...

_____

_____

_____

_____

_____

_____

THE MOST IMPORTANT LESSON THAT MY OTHER PARENT TAUGHT ME WAS...

_____

_____

_____

_____

_____

_____

THE MOST IMPORTANT LESSON THAT MY SIBLINGS TAUGHT ME WAS...

THE MOST IMPORTANT LESSON THAT
MY GRANDPARENTS TAUGHT ME WAS...

WRITE ABOUT THE MOST MEMORABLE DAY WITH YOUR PARENT.

_____
_____
_____
_____
_____
_____

> **FORGETTING IS COMMON**
>
> It's all too common to forget someone's name or an appointment you meant to keep. Information is quickly lost if you don't review it, if you don't want to remember or if it wasn't 'stored' properly in the first case.

WRITE ABOUT THE MOST MEMORABLE DAY WITH YOUR OTHER PARENT.

_____
_____
_____
_____
_____
_____
_____
_____

71 / FAMILY TREE

WRITE ABOUT THE DAY YOUR SIBLING WAS BORN, OR THE FIRST MEMORY YOU HAVE WITH YOUR SIBLING.

_____
_____
_____
_____
_____
_____

WRITE ABOUT THE WORST TIME YOU WERE TOLD OFF BY YOUR PARENTS.

_____
_____
_____
_____
_____
_____
_____

"

THE TRUE ART OF

MEMORY

IS THE ART OF

ATTENTION

— SAMUEL JOHNSON

WHAT IS YOUR FAVOURITE FAMILY STORY?

MY FAVOURITE ACTIVITY TO DO WITH MY PARENT WAS...

___

MY FAVOURITE ACTIVITY TO DO WITH MY PARENT WAS...

___

MY FAVOURITE ACTIVITY TO DO WITH MY SIBLINGS WAS...

_____

_____

_____

_____

_____

_____

_____

> **IT'S ON THE TIP OF MY TONGUE!**
> Have you ever been right on the edge of remembering something? This is called lethologica and is the feeling when you are temporarily unable to access information from your memories. It should come to you eventually!

WHAT IS YOUR BEST KEPT FAMILY SECRET?

_____

_____

_____

_____

_____

_____

_____

_____

_____

WRITE ABOUT A FUNNY
FAMILY STORY THAT HAS BEEN
PASSED DOWN THROUGH GENERATIONS.

CAN YOU REMEMBER YOUR PARENT'S OR GRANDPARENT'S KITCHEN?

Describe it.

DO YOU HAVE QUIRKY OR INTERESTING RELATIVES ON YOUR FAMILY TREE?

Describe one or two of them and what makes them special.

_____
_____
_____
_____
_____
_____

DID YOU GROW UP WITH FAMILY TRADITIONS?

Describe some of them.

_____
_____
_____
_____
_____
_____
_____

DESCRIBE A GAME OR ACTIVITY YOU USED TO PLAY WITH A SIBLING.

_____
_____
_____
_____
_____
_____

> **STRESS**
>
> Stress can be helpful, but high levels of stress affect our memory. When we're under pressure we have difficulties in creating short-term memories and it can also be much harder to learn. This kind of memory loss is temporary and reversible.

WHAT EVENTS HAVE BROUGHT YOU CLOSER TO YOUR FAMILY?

_____
_____
_____
_____
_____
_____
_____
_____

WHAT ARE YOUR FAMILY STORIES OF SACRIFICE?

> So long as the memory of a certain beloved friend lives in my heart, I shall say that

LIFE IS GOOD

— HELEN KELLER

WHAT WAS YOUR RELATIONSHIP LIKE WITH YOUR SIBLINGS?

WHAT WAS YOUR RELATIONSHIP WITH YOUR GRANDPARENTS LIKE?

HOW WAS YOUR RELATIONSHIP WITH AUNTS AND UNCLES?

___

FALSE MEMORIES

Memory is fallible and often these false memories are innocuous. False memories are more serious than 'miss-rememberances' — especially in the case of recollections in criminal investigations.

HOW WAS YOUR RELATIONSHIP WITH YOUR COUSINS?

___

DID YOU FEEL CONNECTED WITH BOTH YOUR PARENTS WHEN YOU WERE GROWING UP, OR ONE MORE THAN THE OTHER?

Why or why not?

_____
_____
_____
_____
_____
_____
_____
_____
_____
_____

DESCRIBE YOUR RELATIONSHIP WITH EACH (OR EITHER) OF YOUR PARENTS WHILE GROWING UP.

What was it like? How did it change as you became an adult?

___
___
___
___
___
___
___
___
___
___

WHAT TRAITS DO YOU SHARE WITH YOUR SIBLINGS, (EITHER CHARACTER OR PHYSICAL)?

In what ways do your traits differ?

_____
_____
_____
_____
_____
_____
_____

DID YOU GET ALONG WITH YOUR SIBLINGS AS A CHILD?

_____
_____
_____
_____
_____
_____
_____

> **FLASHBULB MEMORIES**
>
> There are certain moments in history that everyone remembers where they were when they heard 'the news' due to shock or trauma. Psychologists Roger Brown and James Kulik described these as Flashbulb Memories in 1977.

IN WHAT WAYS HAS YOUR RELATIONSHIP WITH YOUR SIBLINGS CHANGED OVER THE YEARS?

_____
_____
_____
_____
_____
_____

HAVE THERE EVER BEEN ANY SERIOUS ARGUMENTS OR FALL-OUTS BETWEEN YOUR FAMILY MEMBERS?

What happened? Were they ever resolved?

_____
_____
_____
_____
_____
_____
_____

**DESCRIBE THE BIRTH OF
EACH OF YOUR CHILDREN.**

EARLY YEARS

YOUR CHILDHOOD MEMORIES PLAY A HUGE ROLE IN YOUR FUTURE HAPPINESS

DESCRIBE YOUR MOST MEMORABLE BIRTHDAY PARTY AS A CHILD.

> **BAD MEMORIES**
>
> Have you found that your 'bad' memories are the ones that stick in your head? Our brains detect negative information faster in order to keep us safe. We can try to 'unlearn' negative experiences but they leave a strong impression on us.

DID YOU GET ANY AMAZING (OR DISASTROUS) BIRTHDAY CAKES AS A CHILD?

Write about it here.

___

WRITE ABOUT THE FIRST CHRISTMAS THAT YOU CAN REMEMBER.

What happened?

TELL THE STORY OF
THE MOST EMBARRASSING
MOMENT THAT YOU HAD AS A CHILD.

WHAT IS SOMETHING THAT YOU WERE AFRAID OF AS A CHILD?

Describe it. Was there a time it was a particular issue? Did something happen to make you afraid of it?

WHAT IS SOMETHING DIFFICULT THAT YOU HAD TO DO?

Describe what happened.

_____

_____

_____

_____

_____

_____

> **GETTING OLDER**
>
> While memory problems are to be expected as we grow older, remote memory (historic), procedural memory (tasks) and semantic recall (general knowledge) are key preserved memory functions and are less affected by ageing.

WHEN YOU WERE A CHILD, HOW DID YOU IMAGINE YOUR ADULT SELF?

_____

_____

_____

_____

_____

_____

_____

EARLY YEARS

DESCRIBE YOUR FIRST HOME IN AS MUCH DETAIL AS POSSIBLE.

How long did you live there? Why did you move?

___

WHAT WAS YOUR HOUSE LIKE WHEN YOU WERE GROWING UP?

___

> **IF YOU CARRY YOUR CHILDHOOD WITH YOU, YOU NEVER BECOME OLD**

— TOM STOPPARD

WHAT WAS YOUR CHILDHOOD BEDROOM LIKE?

DESCRIBE YOUR FAVOURITE PLACE AS A CHILD.

What was it like and why did you love it?

_____
_____
_____
_____
_____
_____

DESCRIBE YOUR BEST FRIEND WHEN YOU WERE A CHILD.

Write down a story about them.

_____
_____
_____
_____
_____
_____
_____
_____

WHAT WAS YOUR TYPICAL DAY LIKE AS A CHILD?

_____
_____
_____
_____
_____
_____
_____

WHAT WAS YOUR TYPICAL DAY LIKE AS A TEENAGER?

_____
_____
_____
_____
_____
_____
_____

> **SCHOOL DAY MEMORIES**
>
> The period between ages 10-30 has been coined by researchers as the 'reminiscence bump.' We may remember our schools days so vividly because as a teenager we have strong emotions and this creates strong memories.

DESCRIBE YOUR MOST MEMORABLE BIRTHDAY.

> THE MORE OFTEN YOU SHARE WHAT YOU'VE **LEARNED** THE STRONGER THAT INFORMATION WILL BECOME IN YOUR **MEMORY**

— STEVE BRUNKHORST

WHAT DID YOU TYPICALLY DO IN YOUR FAMILY FOR BIRTHDAYS WHEN YOU WERE A CHILD?

WHAT WERE YOUR CHRISTMAS MORNING TRADITIONS WHEN YOU WERE A CHILD?

Do you still do them?

WHAT WAS THE HARDEST PART ABOUT GROWING UP?

_____
_____
_____
_____
_____
_____

> **DIGITAL AMNESIA**
>
> In today's digital age, we have easy access to information, but this might be making it more difficult for us to take in information offline. The Internet has made us learn things differently so when we read a book our brains have to work harder to retain information.

WHAT WAS THE BEST PART ABOUT GROWING UP?

_____
_____
_____
_____
_____
_____
_____
_____

WHAT WORLD EVENTS WERE SIGNIFICANT TO YOU AS A CHILD?

Why were they significant?

WHO LOOKED AFTER YOU MOST OFTEN WHEN YOU WERE A CHILD?

DESCRIBE THE MOST MEMORABLE SLEEPOVER YOU HAD AS A CHILD.

WHO WAS THE MOST MEMORABLE BABYSITTER WHEN YOU WERE A CHILD?

Describe them. What made them memorable?

WHAT WERE YOU MOST PROUD OF AS A CHILD?

> **BLANK SLATE**
>
> Aristotle compared the mind to a blank slate and theorised that humans are born 'blank' and are the sum of their experiences. This theory is not so important today as neuroscientists understand that our memory is an equal mix of nature and nurture.

WHAT WAS THE BEST MOMENT OF YOUR TEENS?

WHEN YOU WERE LITTLE, DID YOU EVER TRY TO RUN AWAY FROM HOME?

What made you want to leave?
What did you pack? How far did you get?

_____
_____
_____
_____
_____
_____
_____
_____
_____
_____

"

There's something known as

Memory Conformity,

also known as

Social Contagion of Memory,

which refers to a situation where one person's telling of a memory influences another person's account of that same experience.

— Rob Roberge

WERE YOU SHY AS A CHILD? BOSSY? OBNOXIOUS?

Describe several of your childhood character traits.
How did those qualities show themselves? Are you still that way?

___

HAVE YOU EVER NEEDED TO BE HOSPITALIZED?

Describe a childhood injury or illness.

BOOKS CAN BE CHILDHOOD FRIENDS.

What were some of your favourites? Why were they special?

_____
_____
_____
_____
_____
_____

WHAT WAS YOUR MOST BELOVED TOY?

Describe its shape, appearance, and texture. What feelings come to mind when you think of that toy?

_____
_____
_____
_____
_____
_____
_____

DO YOU REMEMBER WHAT YOU BOUGHT THE FIRST TIME YOU WERE GIVEN ALLOWANCE/WENT SHOPPING ALONE?

Describe that shopping trip and how it made you feel.

WRITE ABOUT SOME SAYINGS, EXPRESSIONS, OR ADVICE YOU HEARD AT HOME WHEN YOU WERE GROWING UP.

Who said them? What did they mean?
Do you use any of those expressions today?

THINK OF A CHILDHOOD EVENT THAT MADE YOU FEEL ANXIOUS OR SCARED.

Describe both the event itself and the feelings it stirred up.

_____

_____

_____

_____

_____

_____

FORGETTING AS A CHILD

Do you remember your first day of school? Researchers at Emory University found that children up to seven years old could only remember 60% of their early life memories and this decreased to 30% for children up to the age of eight.

WHAT THINGS DID YOU CREATE WHEN YOU WERE A CHILD?

_____

_____

_____

_____

_____

_____

_____

WHAT ARE YOUR HAPPIEST CHILDHOOD MEMORIES?

Describe one event and the feelings associated with it.

_____

_____

_____

_____

_____

_____

WHAT ARE YOUR SADDEST CHILDHOOD MEMORIES?

Describe one event and the feelings associated with it.

_____

_____

_____

_____

_____

_____

WAS THERE A TOY YOU WANTED AS A CHILD BUT NEVER GOT?

Describe why you wanted it so much.

"
MEMORIES ARE LIKE SALT

THE RIGHT AMOUNT BRINGS OUT THE FLAVOUR IN FOOD, TOO MUCH RUINS IT

— PAUL COELHO

WHO INSPIRED YOU MOST AS A CHILD?

Describe why.

_____
_____
_____
_____
_____
_____
_____

> **PUT THE CAMERA AWAY**
>
> Have you ever wondered why people spend more time taking photos than enjoying the moment? Taking a photo of something actually makes our memories worse! Our brains focus on the action instead of what's in the frame!

WHAT IS THE MOST UNCHARACTERISTIC THING YOU DID AS A CHILD?

_____
_____
_____
_____
_____
_____
_____
_____
_____
_____

DO YOU THINK YOU HAD A GOOD CHILDHOOD?

Why do you think this?

_____
_____
_____
_____
_____
_____
_____

> **GAME OF CARDS**
>
> Many master memory champions remember entire decks of cards by making up stories. They associate 'face' cards with characters, then add 'actions' and characters for the number cards until a complete 52-card story is built.

WHAT WAS YOUR FAVOURITE GAME?

_____
_____
_____
_____
_____
_____
_____

WHICH SPORTS DID YOU PLAY?

CAN YOU THINK OF A TIME WHEN YOU MOVED HOME OR SCHOOL AND HOW THIS AFFECTED YOU?

WHAT WERE YOUR FAVOURITE SWEETS OR CHOCOLATES?

> **JOGGING MEMORIES**
>
> When you're having difficulty remembering something there are a number of ways to jog those memories. Listen to music of the time, visit a special place, look at old pictures or get in touch with someone to reminisce.

WHAT WAS YOUR FAVOURITE MAGAZINE?

HOW DID YOU SPEND YOUR WEEKENDS?

> **WHAT MAKES YOU**
>
> People are unique, but we all experience similar things; loss, joy, trauma and love. All of our life events, and the way we react to them, make us who we are. When looking back at memories that 'made' one, remember that you are more than the sum of your past.

WHO WAS YOUR FAVOURITE TEACHER AS A CHILD?

Why did you like them?

IS THERE SOMETHING THAT HAPPENED IN YOUR CHILDHOOD THAT YOU NEED TO FORGIVE YOURSELF FOR?

Why do you find it hard to forgive yourself?

_____
_____
_____
_____
_____
_____
_____
_____
_____
_____

"

WE DO NOT REMEMBER DAYS, WE REMEMBER MOMENTS.

— CESARE PAVESE

WHAT WAS YOUR MOST TRAUMATIC MEMORY AS A CHILD?

DID YOU EVER HAVE A PEN FRIEND?

What country were they from? What did you write to them about?

DID YOU EVER GET LOST ANYWHERE?

What happened?

_____
_____
_____
_____
_____
_____
_____

DID YOU LEARN TO PLAY A MUSICAL INSTRUMENT?

_____
_____
_____
_____
_____
_____

MUSCLE MEMORY

You will have heard the phrase, "it's like riding a bike" in relation to never forgetting a skill. These kind of memory skills are anchored in procedural memory. This kind of memory is more resistant to trauma and is protected deep inside the brain's centre.

**WERE YOU NOT ALLOWED
TO DO SOMETHING THAT YOU REALLY
WANTED TO DO AS A CHILD?**

CAN YOU THINK OF ANY /
CHILDHOOD MEMORIES YOU
WOULD LIKE TO REMEMBER BETTER?

WHAT WAS YOUR FAVOURITE HOBBY WHEN YOU WERE YOUNGER?

THE NIGHT BEFORE...

Have you ever had a bit too much to drink and struggled to remember your evening? You may think you've simply forgotten, but it turns out your brain never recorded those memories — alcohol disrupts our receptors in the hippocampus!

DESCRIBE YOUR FASHION SENSE AS A TEENAGER?

DID YOU EXPERIENCE DEATH OR LOSS AS A CHILD?

How did this experience change you?

_____
_____
_____
_____
_____
_____

HOW DO YOU THINK YOUR CHILDHOOD EXPERIENCES HELPED SHAPE YOUR BEHAVIOUR TODAY?

_____
_____
_____
_____
_____
_____
_____
_____

> **WE COULD NEVER HAVE LOVED THE EARTH SO WELL IF WE HAD HAD NO CHILDHOOD IN IT**
>
> – GEORGE ELIOT

WORK & EDUCATION

HAPPY MEMORIES IN SCHOOL CAN HELP YOU DEVELOP WHO YOU ARE AND WHAT YOU BECOME IN LIFE

DESCRIBE YOUR EARLIEST MEMORY OF SCHOOL.

What happened and how did you feel?
Why do you remember that day? Was it your first day?

___

GASLIGHTING

Gaslighting is a kind of mental abuse. It is when one person lies, presents false information or denies the truth to make their victim doubt their own memories. Gaslighting can affect the victim's self esteem and encourage cognitive dissonance.

DESCRIBE ALL OF THE TEACHERS THAT YOU REMEMBER AT SCHOOL.

DESCRIBE THE MOST MEMORABLE DAY OF SCHOOL IN AS MUCH DETAIL AS YOU CAN.

What happened and how did you feel?

DESCRIBE A SCHOOL PLAY THAT YOU REMEMBER.

What part did you play? Did you enjoy it?

> **TAKE CARE OF ALL YOUR MEMORIES. FOR YOU CANNOT RELIVE THEM.**
>
> – BOB DYLAN

WHAT WAS YOUR FAVOURITE SUBJECT AT SCHOOL?

Describe why.

_____
_____
_____
_____
_____

WHO DID YOU NOT GET ON WELL WITH IN YOUR CLASS?

Why? Describe how they made you feel.

_____
_____
_____
_____
_____
_____

> **IT ONLY TAKES EIGHT SECONDS**
>
> If you really need to remember something try to concentrate on that (and only that) for a full eight seconds. This is the smallest amount of time for information to travel from our long-term memory to the short-term.

WHO WAS THE MOST POPULAR PERSON IN YOUR CLASS?

Describe them. Were you friends with them? Was it you?

_____
_____
_____
_____
_____

WHAT WAS THE WORST THING YOU WERE TOLD OFF FOR IN PRIMARY SCHOOL?

How did it make you feel? Describe what happened.

_____
_____
_____
_____
_____
_____

SHORT-TERM VS LONG-TERM

Short-term memory is retaining short-term information, for example, what you're doing with a pen in your hand. Long-term memory is accessing memories from the past, for example, the name of your first teacher.

WHAT WAS YOUR FAVOURITE SCHOOL TRIP?

Describe everything that happened.

DESCRIBE A MEMORABLE SCHOOL EVENT.

(prom, sports day, a fayre..) Why was it memorable?

DID YOU WIN ANY AWARDS AT SCHOOL?

What were they for? How did winning them make you feel?
If you didn't win any, how did that make you feel?

___

DID YOU GO TO UNIVERSITY?

Describe your first few days there.

___

WHAT WAS YOUR UNIVERSITY EXPERIENCE LIKE OVERALL?

Did you enjoy it?

_____
_____
_____
_____
_____
_____
_____

> **MNEMOSYNE**
>
> Greek goddess Mnemosyne, was the goddess of memory. She was a Titaness and the daughter of Uranus (Heaven) and Gaea (Earth), and was also the mother of the nine Muses (with Zeus). These Muses were the primary godessess of the arts and sciences.

WRITE ABOUT YOUR UNIVERSITY FRIENDS.

Describe them all. Do you still keep in touch?

_____
_____
_____
_____
_____
_____
_____
_____

DESCRIBE YOUR GRADUATION

How did you feel? Who came to watch?

> "THERE IS NO WAY I CAN JUST ERASE THOSE MEMORIES. THAT WOULD BE THE SAME AS ERASING MY OWN SELF.

— HARUKI MURAKAMI

DESCRIBE YOUR EARLIEST MEMORY OF WORKING.

What was the job? Did you enjoy it? Why do you remember that day?

_____
_____
_____
_____
_____
_____

DESCRIBE THE EARLIEST JOB INTERVIEW THAT YOU CAN REMEMBER.

What was it for? Did you get it?

_____
_____
_____
_____
_____
_____
_____

DESCRIBE THE WORST JOB INTERVIEW THAT YOU EVER HAD.

What made it so bad? Did you get the job?

_____
_____
_____
_____
_____
_____

WHAT WAS THE WORST JOB THAT YOU EVER HAD?

Describe it.

_____
_____
_____
_____
_____
_____

> **GET DOODLING**
>
> While it may feel that doodling in a meeting or listening to a lecture was a sign of not paying attention it has been proven recently that doodling helps improve information retention! In a way, doodling keeps your brain active so it doesn't wander.

WHAT WAS THE BEST JOB THAT YOU EVER HAD?

Describe it.

_____
_____
_____
_____
_____
_____
_____
_____
_____
_____

FRIENDS, RELATIONSHIPS & LATER LIFE

MEMORIES OF GROWING UP AND OUR RELATIONSHIPS PLAY A HUGE ROLE IN SHAPING WHO WE ARE

DESCRIBE THE FIRST HOLIDAY THAT YOU WENT ON WITHOUT YOUR PARENTS.

Who did you go with and where did you go?

DESCRIBE THE SCARIEST MEMORY YOU HAD ON A PLANE.

DESCRIBE YOUR FIRST EVER DATE.

Who did you go with and where did you go? Did it go well?

_____
_____
_____
_____
_____
_____

MIND HACKS

If you consider your memory to be a bad one, and that you are constantly forgetting things, try this long-term brain hack. Tell yourself regularly that you have a good memory — in a way this kind of coaching or mantra is a self-fulfilling prophecy.

DESCRIBE YOUR FIRST DATE WITH YOUR CURRENT PARTNER.

_____
_____
_____
_____
_____
_____
_____
_____

DESCRIBE THE MOMENT
THAT YOU KNEW THAT YOU LOVED
YOUR CURRENT PARTNER.

> **MEMORY IS A WAY OF TELLING YOU WHAT'S IMPORTANT TO YOU**
>
> – SALMAN RUSHDIE

DESCRIBE THE FIRST CHRISTMAS THAT YOU REMEMBER AS AN ADULT WITH YOUR OWN FAMILY.

_____
_____
_____
_____
_____
_____
_____

WHAT IS YOUR MOST EMBARRASSING STORY AS AN ADULT?

_____
_____
_____
_____
_____
_____

> **ANCIENT STORYTELLERS**
>
> Ancient Vikings had a professional class of storytellers who shared history and mythology memorised in their heads. The Skalds, as they were known, were integral in passing Viking culture down from generation to generation.

ARE YOU MARRIED?

Describe your wedding day.

___

DESCRIBE YOUR FAVOURITE PLACE AS AN ADULT.

Why do you like it? Do you go often?

DISCUSS WHO INSPIRED YOU MOST AS YOU MATURED.

WHAT WAS THE BEST MOMENT OF YOUR 20s?

WHAT WAS THE BEST MOMENT OF YOUR 30s?

HOW DID YOU MEET YOUR SIGNIFICANT OTHER?

Describe it in as much detail as possible

> **FAMILY FOLKLORE**
>
> We are often told stories of our parents' childhoods or tales of the war from our grandparents and great grandparents. All of these stories make up a shared sense of identity and give us easily remembered roots, keeping memories alive.

DID YOU HAVE MANY BOYFRIENDS/GIRLFRIENDS GROWING UP?

Discuss some of them.

_____
_____
_____
_____
_____
_____
_____

WHAT ARE YOU MOST PROUD OF AS AN ADULT?

_____
_____
_____
_____
_____
_____
_____

"

SOMETIMES YOU WILL NEVER KNOW THE VALUE OF A MOMENT UNTIL IT BECOMES A MEMORY

— DR SEUSS

WHERE IS THE MOST FASCINATING PLACE THAT YOU HAVE EVER VISITED?

Describe it. Why is it so fascinating to you?

DESCRIBE YOUR FAVOURITE HOLIDAY IN AS MUCH DETAIL AS POSSIBLE.

> **REMEMBER REMEMBER**
>
> You would think that the more you think of a memory, the easier it is to remember it? In many cases that just isn't the case. Researchers at UCLA believe that the longer you let a memory fade before retrieving it, the stronger it will be!

TALK ABOUT BEING ABROAD AND TRYING NEW CUISINE AND CULTURES.

Describe what you experienced and how it made you feel

WHAT IS ONE THING ABOUT TODAY THAT YOU NEVER WANT TO FORGET?

> **AMNESIA IN POPULAR CULTURE**
>
> Amnesia has been used as a plot point in popular culture since the early 20th century. It's important to note that a second knock on the head will not cure amnesia — no matter how many times you've seen it happen on TV.

DESCRIBE THE MOST UNUSUAL OR MEMORABLE PLACE YOU HAVE EVER LIVED.

THINK OF A TIME WHEN YOU DID SOMETHING YOU SHOULDN'T HAVE DONE.

Describe both the incident and the feelings they created.

WHAT'S THE BEST GIFT YOU'VE EVER GIVEN OR RECEIVED?

Describe the circumstances.

WHAT'S THE MOST MEMORABLE THING YOU EVER GOT IN THE MAIL?

Describe it. Do you know who sent it?

WHAT NICKNAMES HAVE YOU EVER BEEN GIVEN?

Who gave you them? Did you like them?

WHAT 'MUNDANE MOMENTS' FROM YOUR LIFE MIGHT MAKE GREAT ESSAY MATERIAL?

Describe them.

_____
_____
_____
_____
_____
_____

WHAT ARE THE MOST MEMORABLE WORKS OF VISUAL ART YOU HAVE SEEN?

Describe them. How did they make you feel?

_____
_____
_____
_____
_____
_____

BRAIN EXPERIMENTS

Wilder Penfield, an American-Canadian neurosurgeon, used electrical currents to stimulate the brain during surgery while his patients were still awake. He discovered that you could evoke a memory merely by stimulating parts of the cortex.

> **MEMORY IS THE DIARY THAT WE ALL CARRY AROUND WITH US**
>
> — OSCAR WILDE

DID YOU HAVE ANY BAD HABITS?

When did you grow out of these?

WHAT WAS THE WORST ACCIDENT YOU EVER HAD?

Who was there? Describe the emotions that you felt and how you got through it.

WHEN WAS THE FIRST TIME YOU KISSED SOMEONE?

Can you describe the situation?

HAVE YOU HAD ANY RECURRING DREAMS OR NIGHTMARES?

Describe them and how they made you feel.

_____
_____
_____
_____
_____

> **EUPHORIC RECALL**
>
> This is a psychological term relating to people remembering past experiences in a positive light. Some people overlook the negative and become obsessed with recreating pleasurable memories — whether or not they are accurate.

WRITE ABOUT A TIME YOU FAILED AT SOMETHING.

How did this make you feel? What do you think you learned from it?

_____
_____
_____
_____
_____
_____
_____

RECALL AN IMPORTANT TIME IN YOUR LIFE WHEN YOU MADE A FRESH START OR TRIED SOMETHING NEW FOR THE VERY FIRST TIME.

THE CONNECTIONS WE FORM WITH PEOPLE ARE CENTRAL TO HOW WE LIVE OUR LIVES.

Think of a relationship in your life, past or present. How might the course of your life be different if you hadn't made that connection?

_____
_____
_____
_____
_____
_____
_____
_____
_____
_____

IT'S 100 YEARS IN THE FUTURE. SOMEONE JUST DUG UP A TIME CAPSULE OF YOUR LIFE.

Describe the items inside it and what you hope they communicate about you. Tie each item back to a memory from your life.

DÉJÀ VU

Many of us have had the undeniable feeling that something you're experiencing has happened before. Déjà vu (French for 'already lived') is more than a memory illusion. Your brain is in fact trying to correct an inaccurate memory and is fact-checking you!

DO YOU HAVE ANY SCARS?

What memories are attached to them?

_____

_____

_____

_____

_____

> **REMEMBERING PAIN**
>
> Researchers at McGill University in Canada have found that men and women remember pain very differently. Studies showed that women were more sensitive to pain, but were less stressed by the memory of that pain.

THINK OF AN ORDINARY RITUAL YOU PERFORM EVERY DAY.

Taking a walk, drinking your coffee, checking the news, stretching. It can be anything you do on a regular basis that is important to you. What are your earliest memories involving this ritual? Has it shaped other areas of your life? Why do you think this particular one became so important to you?

_____

_____

_____

_____

_____

_____

FIND A FAVOURITE PHOTOGRAPH FROM YOUR PAST.

Study every element of the photo and try to remember what you were thinking and feeling. What is it about this photograph that makes it stand out as a favourite? Do you experience any unexpected emotions when you look at it?

> "
> # A MEMORY IS A BEAUTIFUL THING, IT'S ALMOST A DESIRE THAT YOU MISS
>
> — GUSTAVE FLAUBERT

THINK BACK TO WHEN YOU WERE YOUNGER.

Did you have any skills you've lost over time?

WHAT FOOD HAS MADE FREQUENT APPEARANCES IN YOUR LIFE?

Maybe your family has a favourite dish, special dessert, or notable recipe. Revisit memories where food makes an appearance. Is there a common thread? Also consider how your point of view changes in each memory you revisit.

THINK OF A TIME YOUR LOYALTIES PULLED YOU IN DIFFERENT DIRECTIONS

A clash with family members over politics, religion, or being stuck between feuding friends. What elements made you identify with one side or the other?

JAMAIS VU

Jamais vu (French for 'never seen') is when our brains fail to recognise something that should be familiar and it's disorientating. Put this to the test by writing a common word down as many times as you can in two minutes. Does the word still look correct?

WRITE ABOUT THE FRIEND OR FRIENDS THAT HAVE HAD THE MOST IMPACT ON YOUR LIFE.

Describe them and recall your favourite memories about them.

WRITE LETTERS

HAND WRITE LETTERS TO ACTIVATE MORE AREAS OF THE BRAIN AND HELP IMPROVE YOUR MEMORY

187 / WRITE LETTERS